W9-CKT-158

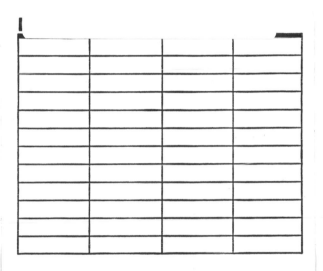

ELIE WIESEL

SPEAKING OUT AGAINST GENOCIDE

SARAH MACHAJEWSKI

ROSEN
PUBLISHING®

Published in 2015 by The Rosen Publishing Group, Inc.
29 East 21st Street, New York, NY 10010

First Edition

Library of Congress Cataloging-in-Publication Data

Machajewski, Sarah.
Elie Wiesel: speaking out against genocide/Sarah Machajewski.
    pages cm.—(A documentary history of the Holocaust)
Includes bibliographical references and index.
ISBN 978-1-4777-7609-4 (library bound)
1. Wiesel, Elie, 1928– 2. Jews—Romania—Biography. 3. Jewish authors—
Biography. 4. Authors, French—20th century—Biography. 5. Holocaust
survivors—Biography. 6. Holocaust, Jewish (1939–1945—Influence. 7.
Genocide—Prevention. I. Title.
DS135.R73W5447 2014
940.53'18092—dc23
[B]

2013049325

Manufactured in the United States of America

CONTENTS

INTRODUCTION

Elie Wiesel is a highly sought-after public speaker because he conveys a powerful message of tolerance and justice.

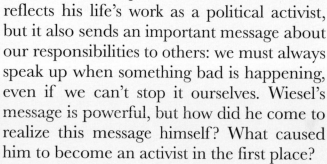

Elie Wiesel, winner of the 1986 Nobel Peace Prize, closed his acceptance speech by stating, "There may be times when we are powerless to prevent injustice, but there must never be a time when we fail to protest." Wiesel's statement reflects his life's work as a political activist, but it also sends an important message about our responsibilities to others: we must always speak up when something bad is happening, even if we can't stop it ourselves. Wiesel's message is powerful, but how did he come to realize this message himself? What caused him to become an activist in the first place?

Elie Wiesel came of age during one of the world's darkest moments: World War II and the Nazi occupation of Europe. Under the direction of dictator Adolf Hitler, Germany's army carried out a mass genocide against several ethnic groups, particularly Jews. From 1933 to 1945, Jews in Germany and Nazi-occupied Europe were discriminated against, abused, sent to concentration camps, and eventually murdered, simply because of their ethnic and religious background. This period is now known as the Holocaust. Born Jewish in Eastern Europe before the Nazi occupation, young Elie had no way of knowing that one day he would lose his family, friends, home, and faith because of unexplainable hatred.

At the age of fifteen, Elie and his family were transported from their home to a concentration camp. By the age of sixteen, he had suffered through extreme starvation, hard labor, and the death of his mother, father, and sister. In only a few years, everything he had ever known—from his faith in God to his faith in man—was taken from him. And yet, despite his experiences, Wiesel has come to be regarded as a public champion of justice, tolerance, and acceptance.

Perhaps the most surprising thing about Wiesel's activism is that he initially refused to get involved. After the war ended, he rarely spoke about his experiences in his private life, let alone in front of the world. He has said that the words needed to describe such a horrific experience don't even exist. However, Wiesel also recognized that the Holocaust happened because the world stood by silently. Millions of innocent people, including about six million Jews, lost their lives in a genocide that could possibly have been prevented. Horrified at the thought of this ever happening again, Wiesel decided that his powerful story—shared through writing, education, and general activism—could be used to show what happens when we don't speak out against injustice.

Though he was originally reluctant, Wiesel turned his tragedy into a teaching experience. The success of his literary works gave him a platform and a voice, and his continued fame has allowed him to dedicate his life to education and fighting injustice. Over the past seventy years, Wiesel's life story and his fights against genocide, indifference, and injustice remind us why we should never forget the Holocaust's cautionary lessons.

ELIE'S EARLY YEARS

Eliezer "Elie" Wiesel was born on September 30, 1928, in Sighet, Transylvania. This area is now a part of Romania. Elie's parents, Shlomo and Sarah, both grew up in Sighet; they married and chose to stay and have a family there. The third child in a family of four, Elie had two older sisters, Hilda and Beatrice, and one younger sister, Tzipora. The Wiesel family spoke many languages in their home. Though Yiddish was what they spoke most often, Elie also knew German, Hungarian, and Romanian.

Elie's childhood was a relatively normal one: His family was very close, he went to school, and he enjoyed spending time with his friends. But there were two major factors that determined his fate during the Holocaust: his religion and his location.

A JEWISH UPBRINGING

Religion was a defining feature of Elie's upbringing. The Wiesels were Hasidic Jews, which means they believed in Hasidism, a branch of Orthodox Judaism. Orthodox Jews' lives are guided by Jewish teachings

Wiesel's home in Sighet, located in present-day Romania, was the background for many happy childhood memories. Today, it has been turned into a museum for the public.

and practices, and their beliefs are based on a traditional interpretation of their faith.

Elie's beliefs were greatly influenced by his religious family. Family members of varying devotion surrounded him. His mother was deeply religious and encouraged her son to be so, too. Elie's father was religious, but he was also open to modern ideas. He made sure Elie studied modern Hebrew so that he could keep up with contemporary events. In an interview with the Academy of Achievement, Wiesel said, "My father taught me how to reason, how to reach my mind. My soul belonged to my grandfather and my mother." The different approaches defined his childhood and stayed with him throughout his life. Wiesel has maintained his deep religious beliefs, and he has employed the skills his father taught him to be successful in his work and other aspects of his life.

Wiesel's maternal grandfather, Dodye Feig, was perhaps the biggest influence on him. Feig was a devout Hasidic Jew and deeply respected in Sighet because he was an active member of his community. In his younger years, he helped a group of Polish Jews on the run. Though nobody knows for sure, it is thought that they were trying to escape persecution for their beliefs. At the time, helping these people escape was a crime, and Feig found himself in jail because of it. His grandfather's devoutness and determination to help others in need had an enormous impact on the young Elie.

The family's sense of traditionalism was incorporated into every part of Elie's life, from his home environment to what he learned at school. In fact, thanks to his grandfather's influence, Elie went to a yeshiva, an academy of Jewish learning. As a student at a Hasidic yeshiva, he focused mainly on a body of religious texts known as the Talmud. In his adult life, Wiesel would go on to write books about what the Talmud and his faith meant to him and how they influenced his view of what happened during the Holocaust.

A yeshiva is very different from a nonreligious school. Most of the students' time is spent praying and thinking about the meaning of religious texts. The idea is that through prayer and intelligent thinking about one's beliefs, the believer can be closer to God. With most of his free time spent in prayers and contemplation, faith was a dominating force in Elie's life. His relationship with God was something he struggled greatly with while living through the Holocaust.

SIGHET: A QUIET COMMUNITY

Sighet was a tiny rural village at the base of the Transylvanian Alps. When Wiesel was a teenager, the population reached a height of about twenty-seven thousand people. The village was so small that it wasn't even included on most maps. However, despite its size, its residents were content to live in a place that preserved traditional ways of life.

Sighet was far enough from the country's major cities that the villagers' lives were undisturbed by urban activity,

Wiesel told the *New York Times* that it is "impossible to contain the emotions" when he returns to Sighet and the home he grew up in.

but it was close enough for news and current events to reach the residents. Thanks to Dodye Feig's reputation and the family's roots in Sighet, Wiesel's family was deeply immersed in their community. In fact, Sighet was so small that it would have been almost impossible to be uninvolved in the town's happenings.

Families settled in Sighet and stayed for generations. A large portion of Sighet's residents were Jewish, which gave the town a distinct identity. The town's Jewish population formed through immigration, and over time, the town became the center of cultural and political life for its Jewish residents.

In the 2002 documentary *Elie Wiesel: First Person Singular*, Wiesel reflected upon what life was like in Sighet. Many of Sighet's residents were modern Jews. They worked in shops, offices, schools, and synagogues while also practicing their faith. Similarly, many yeshiva students divided their time between studying their religion and learning how to weave and perform other trades.

Growing up in a village like Sighet instilled in Wiesel an appreciation for both the past and the present. It represented everything that "home" should be, given his family's roots and the sense of identity and belonging he found there. Because of this, Wiesel has always looked back on Sighet fondly. In *Elie Wiesel: First Person Singular*, he remarked, "Why is it that my town still enchants me so? Is it because in my memory it is entangled with my childhood? In all my novels it serves as background and vantage point. In my fantasy I still see myself in it."

For years the quiet village remained somewhat of a dream to him. Being forced traumatically out of his home at a young age only reinforced his sense of longing for the happy life he once knew.

CHANGE COMES TO EUROPE

Elie's childhood was quiet and peaceful. However, elsewhere in Europe, major changes began happening that would eventually determine Elie's fate and the fate of six million other Jews. Though it took twelve years for the effects to actually reach Sighet, significant events in the early 1930s put the wheels in motion for what would eventually become state-sponsored genocide.

Signs of change began surfacing in Europe as early as 1933. A little over a decade after World War I, most of Europe had been in a state of financial and social recovery from the war. Germany was one of the hardest-hit countries because it was seen as the war's primary aggressor. With the end of World War I in 1919, the Allied powers signed the Treaty of Versailles, which forced Germany to accept all blame. The rigid terms included a limit to the size of its army (capped at one hundred thousand members) and financial consequences. These were so taxing on the German state that the economy experienced a depression.

Germany's depressed economy took a toll on its citizens, who grew increasingly unsatisfied with their government. At the same time, a man named Adolf Hitler began formulating a plan to take over the German government. He also published writings about his political ideas in a book titled *Mein Kampf*. In two volumes published in 1925 and 1926, Hitler wrote that Germans were racially superior to all other groups of people. He specifically targeted Jews as a problem for the nation, theorizing that they were racially "inferior." He argued that their mere existence prevented Germany—and the world—from being racially pure. Hitler believed Germany could

AN "INFERIOR" RACE

Judaism is one of the world's oldest religions. There isn't one definitive answer on what makes someone a Jew, or how a Jewish person should look, feel, think, or act. As such, there's no specific trait that separates Jews from any other group of people. Why, then, did Hitler and the Nazis believe that Jews were "inferior" to other people?

According to the U.S. Holocaust Memorial Museum, Hitler believed the key to understanding the world was to understand all human history as a struggle between the races. Hitler attributed positive and negative characteristics to groups of people and argued that these traits were a result of irrefutable biology. He also thought that because space on Earth was limited, different races would always be competing to gain *Lebensraum*, or "living space," for their own kind. It was this line of thinking that led Hitler to determine that no one race could have true power unless all others were eradicated. Though Judaism is technically a religion, Hitler identified the Jewish people as a race.

Hitler and his followers identified Jews as the German people's ultimate enemy, blaming them for ruining German purity and strength. After gaining power in 1933, the Nazi Party put its anti-Semitic beliefs into practice. The Nazis launched a propaganda campaign of racist stereotypes against Jews. They then passed a series of laws to remove Jews from any governmental position or role that they believed would undermine German progress.

Though today we look back at these ideologies and say they are wrong, at the time, many people latched on to the Nazi Party's agenda. Nothing about Hitler's beliefs was rooted in fact, yet he and his party became powerful enough to create and propagate race theories out of thin air. Unfortunately, because of his unchecked power, Hitler turned his own unjustifiable racism into state-sponsored genocide.

never fully achieve racial purity—and become a revitalized nation—as long as Jews were around.

Hitler spent many years gathering support and conceiving of a plan to turn his ideologies into actions. In January 1933, he found his opportunity. Hitler was appointed chancellor of Germany, backed by the Nazi Party. With money, an army, and authority at his fingertips, he began laying the groundwork for a state unlike anything seen before in

After coming to power in Germany, Adolf Hitler (*left*) carried out policies of state-sponsored racism and then genocide. He had the help of high-ranking Nazi officials such as Hermann Göring (*right*).

modern Europe. Germany's laws, education, economy, and culture all came under Nazi rule, and citizens were forced to abide by the orders of the government.

Hitler and his government made swift changes to Germany's legislation and soon passed several laws outlawing all other political parties. This turned Hitler's chancellorship into a dictatorship, and soon he had the ability to rule unchecked by any outside force. In 1935, he decreed the Nuremberg Race Laws, which denied Jews their German citizenship, effectively making them second-class citizens. Then Jews were eliminated from public office, government agencies, teaching, and other positions of cultural importance.

Meanwhile, hundreds of miles away in Sighet, a young Elie Wiesel went about his life unaffected by the state-sponsored racism. Nobody knew then that these unjust practices would soon creep into the far corners of Eastern Europe and bring with them a horrific genocide that aimed to purge the country, and soon most of Europe, of its Jewish population.

CHAPTER 2

THE WORLD REMAINS SILENT

As the 1930s passed, news began reaching Sighet regarding the treatment of Jews in Germany. Hearing rumblings of Jews having their homes and businesses attacked, being removed from their professions and schools, and being forcibly displaced from their homes was troubling, but few people truly believed what they heard. Many thought the news was exaggerated or untrue. In his book *Night*, Wiesel suggests that people's refusal to acknowledge the facts before them was not necessarily ignorance a failure of imagination: it showed they couldn't imagine people were capable of committing the more horrific acts that were to come.

Though the Nazi Party had assumed power in Germany in 1933, for a number of years Sighet remained relatively unaffected by the developments in that country. Then, in 1939, Germany invaded Poland. This aggressive act began World War II. As Germany advanced across Europe, it left in its wake ruin, death, and horrific crimes against humanity. Unfortunately for Elie and the other Jews in Sighet, they would eventually be swept up in the storm.

GHETTO AND DEPORTATION

Shlomo Wiesel was a shopkeeper and well-respected community leader—two things that made him aware of news that passed through town. He made sure his son was exposed to news and current events despite the fact that they were relatively far from Budapest, the country's capital. The Wiesel family heard snippets of information about what was going on, but as they were not yet experiencing it themselves, they still led normal lives.

With Germany's invasion of other nations came the reordering of territories belonging to other countries. When Elie was a boy, Sighet belonged to Transylvania and then Romania. In 1940, Sighet became a part of Hungary, which soon allied itself with Germany in the hopes of preserving its independence.

In 1941, the Hungarian government decided to deport Polish and Russian Jews living in the country and hand them over to the Nazis. Wiesel describes this in his book *Night*. In the book, one person who was forced to leave was Moishe, a local pauper. Moishe escaped his captors and returned to Sighet to warn the residents. Moishe acted as a witness, saying that Jews around Europe were being forced to dig their own graves before being executed by the Gestapo, the Nazis' special police. The town's residents did not believe Moishe's story. In Wiesel's view, had Sighet's residents believed the testimony of people like Moishe, they may have been able to escape.

Later in the war, the Hungarian government attempted to pull out of its alliance with Germany. In March 1944, German troops invaded Hungary and the Hungarian government fell to Germany. It was only a short time before the country's Jews felt the implications of Hitler's genocidal plan. Because Sighet was so far removed from Budapest, many residents believed Nazi actions would not reach them. However, the Germans did invade the small village and forced a series of oppressive measures upon the town's Jews. Community leaders were arrested, Jews were forced to hand over their most valuable possessions, and all Jews were required to wear a yellow Star of David somewhere on their clothing.

Elie, at only fifteen years old, looked to his father for guidance about how to respond. Shlomo advised him to wear the

Jews in German-occupied countries were forced to wear the yellow Star of David. It identified them as Jews and caused many to feel like second-class citizens, as Hitler intended.

yellow star with pride and not let these actions make him feel like less of a person. He argued that if that was the extent of how bad the situation would be, the family would be able to get through it. However, as time went on, it became increasingly apparent that the rumors they had heard were not untrue ramblings.

Shortly after these measures were put into effect, the German police ordered Hungary's Jews to be confined to small ghettos. Ghettos often encompassed only a few small blocks, and families were forced to live together despite the lack of room. Many residents knew that this would be bad, but they still thought it would just be a matter of time before life returned to normal. However, as Wiesel describes in *Night*, the ghettos were just a place to contain the country's Jews before they were deported to concentration camps. The young Elie did not know that the time spent in the ghetto would be the last time his entire family would be together.

A-7713

On May 6, 1944, Elie, his family, and Sighet's Jews were deported from their tiny village. They spent three days in crowded railcars with limited water and barely any food. Wiesel wrote in his memoir *All Rivers Run to the Sea*, "The time in the cattle car was the death of my adolescence." After a few hundred miles, the trains passed through Hungary, Slovakia, and then Poland. They arrived at the Auschwitz-Birkenau concentration camp. Any doubts about what they would soon face were quickly squashed.

Auschwitz opened in 1940 in southern Poland. It was the largest of all the Nazi death camps. Jews who passed through Auschwitz were divided into two categories in a process known as *Selektion*. Young, able-bodied people were sent to

"ARBEIT MACHT FREI"

On a midsized plot of land in southern Poland, squat brick buildings stand surrounded by iron fencing and barbed wire. Cold, desolate, and alone, the military-style buildings blend in with the surrounding area's industrial feel. But these buildings are not just former factories. They're Auschwitz, the most notorious of the Nazi death camps and a standing symbol of the Holocaust.

The camp opened as a place to house political prisoners but evolved into a huge extermination complex that functioned to carry out Hitler's "Final Solution." Arriving prisoners were greeted by the German phrase "Arbeit Macht Frei" as they passed through the camp's iron gates. In English, the phrase means, "Work Sets You Free." The phrase was a mockery of what awaited the prisoners. They labored in factories on the ground to produce supplies for Germany's war effort, but there were no intentions of ever freeing them: the complex also had prison barracks, gas chambers, and crematoriums.

Auschwitz prisoners slept in rat- and lice-infested barracks and contracted dysentery, typhus, tuberculosis, and malaria. They were given stale bread and thin cotton uniforms to wear year-round, even in winter. The prisoners were starving, emaciated, weak, and abused. Life expectancy at Auschwitz (and other concentration camps) was no more than four months.

In addition to the slave labor and mass killings, SS physicians, including the most notorious, Josef Mengele, selected thousands of Auschwitz prisoners to be part of barbaric medical experiments. He sterilized prisoners, performed operations without anesthetic, and maimed living bodies to see if he could learn about genetics in the interest of creating an Aryan "super race."

Soviet troops liberated Auschwitz in January 1945. According to the U.S. Holocaust Memorial Museum, approximately

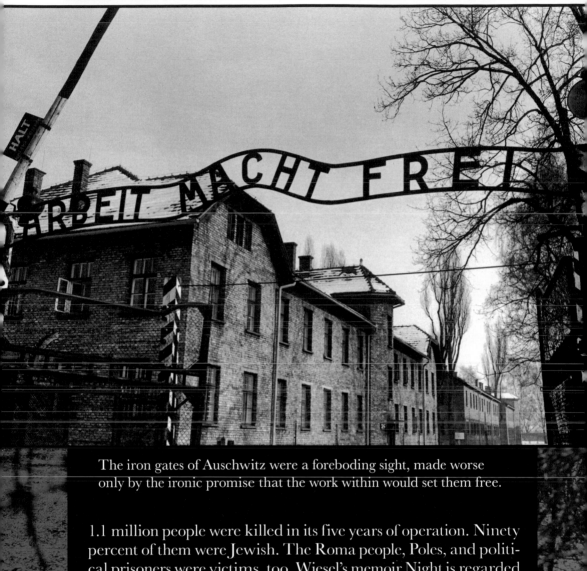

The iron gates of Auschwitz were a foreboding sight, made worse only by the ironic promise that the work within would set them free.

1.1 million people were killed in its five years of operation. Ninety percent of them were Jewish. The Roma people, Poles, and political prisoners were victims, too. Wiesel's memoir Night is regarded as an important source of information on life inside Auschwitz. His activism, as well as efforts of the United Nations, has kept the site open for people around the world to learn about the crimes that took place within its walls.

Thousands of Hungarian Jews arrive at Auschwitz in June 1944. The Wiesel family had arrived only one month before this photo was taken.

work. The weak, sick, and old were sent to die in the gas chambers.

When the trains arrived at Auschwitz, Elie and his family got off the railcar and passed through the camp's iron gates. Another passenger on the train had told Elie and his father to lie about their ages (to appear older and younger, respectively) in order to have the best chance of survival. The Schutzstaffel (also known as SS) guards examined Elie and Shlomo and let them pass, making them prisoners of the camp. Elie had an inmate number tattooed on his left arm. He was no longer a person, but a number: A-7713. The tattoo remains there to this day.

Elie and his father did not know that on the other side of the camp, the rest of their family's fate was being determined. Elie's two older sisters, Hilda and Beatrice, were allowed to live. Elie's mother and seven-year-old sister, Tzipora, were sent to

Auschwitz, like most concentration camps, was surrounded by barbed wire—a message to prisoners that they could not escape.

the gas chambers. Elie never saw them again.

Conditions inside the camps were brutal. Prisoners were starved and beaten, yet expected to perform hard labor in the camp's factories, often to the point of collapse. They were shot if they spoke out or resisted. They were gassed to death if they became unable to work.

Elie and his father remained by each other's side while in the camp. Shlomo was older and weakened more quickly than his son. Elie felt responsible for ensuring their survival. Elie told Oprah Winfrey in 2006, "I was the wrong person [to survive]. I was always timid, frightened, bashful. I had never taken any initiative to try to live. I never pushed myself, never volunteered. I was the wrong person. I was always sick when I was a child. I got here, and if I survived this place until Buchenwald, it was because my father was alive. And I knew that if I died, he would die."

NIGHT BEGINS

At the young age of fifteen, Elie Wiesel lost his home, his family, his identity, and any sense of comfort or safety from his old life. The atrocities around him nearly made him lose his faith in humanity. According to *Night*, his first memoir, he "began to hate." One thing that sustained him initially was his faith in God. A devout believer from a young age, Elie turned to God for answers. How could a loving God subject his people to something so evil? His faith sustained him, until one event almost caused him to cast off his faith entirely.

The SS gathered Auschwitz's prisoners in the camp's yard, where they witnessed the shooting death of a fellow prisoner. During the march back to their barracks, Elie saw a child hanging from the gallows in the yard. He said that this moment, the hanging of an innocent child, was the lowest point of his faith in God. In *Night*, Wiesel wrote, "Behind me, I heard the same man asking: 'Where is God now?' And I heard a voice within me answer him, 'Where is He? Here He is—He is hanging here on this gallows.'"

The Holocaust was so horrific that it deeply challenged Wiesel's faith in both God and man. Yet, he

Auschwitz had dedicated execution areas. This execution wall is located between prisoner barracks.

maintained his beliefs even in his darkest hour and remained committed to Judaism throughout his life. In an interview on the public television show *Richard Heffner's Open Mind*, Wiesel explained, "It's a wounded faith, but it's there."

27

LIBERATION, AT LAST

As 1944 progressed, Germany's army started weakening on both the eastern and western fronts. Facing increasing pressure from the Allies, Hitler and the Nazis grew nervous that they were losing the war. This did not deter them from their plan. In fact, they increased their efforts to kill as many Jews as possible. In August 1944, Elie and his father were transferred to Buna, a labor camp a few miles from the main Auschwitz site. Conditions worsened, and Elie's life revolved around two things: finding food and staying alive.

After a few months in Buna, the prisoners began hearing cannons somewhere off in the distance. The Germans prepared to evacuate the camp, fleeing in the opposite direction of advancing Soviet forces.

Elie had just undergone an operation on his foot, which became infected from the camp's poor sanitary conditions. The SS prepared to evacuate the camp, and the camp's doctor gave Elie a choice to stay in the camp's infirmary or to evacuate with the other prisoners. Elie believed that anybody left behind would be executed immediately. Elie and his father decided to evacuate, thinking it was their best chance for survival. In January 1945,

Allied forces liberated Buchenwald in Germany in 1945. This picture shows some of the concentration camp's weak and emaciated survivors.

they and thousands of other inmates were sent on a death march from Buna to a town called Gleiwitz. The prisoners marched for days in the snow in thin uniforms, sometimes without shoes. The guards forced them to run and shot anyone who stopped.

Wiesel stands in front of a photo of himself and other prisoners taken while he was in the Buchenwald concentration camp. He is pictured in the bottom right-hand corner.

Upon arrival, the prisoners were shipped in a railcar to Buchenwald, a concentration camp in Germany. About twenty thousand prisoners left Buna, but only six thousand reached Buchenwald. Elie and Shlomo Wiesel were among them.

A few months into their time at Buchenwald, Elie's father contracted dysentery. Elie traded his rations of bread to sleep near him. Weak, emaciated, and dying, Shlomo Wiesel cried out into the night for his son to help him. Terrified of being punished by the guards, Elie lay silent in the bunk above his father and pretended not to hear him. Because Shlomo would not be quiet, the guards beat him into submission. Elie heard the entire thing but could not utter a sound. The guards took Shlomo to the infirmary where he died, three short weeks before liberation. Elie never saw him again.

The Allies defeated Germany in the spring of 1945. Buchenwald was liberated on April 11. Elie was sixteen years old. He was sick, alone, and orphaned by the Holocaust.

By the end of World War II, six million Jews had lost their lives at the hands of the Nazis. According to the BBC, approximately five million other civilians, such as the Roma, Poles, homosexuals, and political prisoners, were also murdered. The Holocaust claimed eleven million innocent lives in a display of the deadliest state-sponsored genocide the world had ever seen.

A VOW OF SILENCE

Without a home, family, or country, Elie was sent to an orphanage in France with other Jewish children.

There, he had to choose between secular studies or religious studies. In the documentary *Elie Wiesel: First Person Singular*, Wiesel points out that though his trust in God had been severely wounded by the Holocaust, he returned to his faith. He said, "My only experience in the secular world was Auschwitz."

The remainder of Elie's youth became a process of finding a new normal. He had witnessed unspeakable things, but he had survived. Part of his survival was learning how to integrate back into normal society. He questioned his identity: Why had he survived? Why had his parents and friends died? Could a tragedy of this magnitude happen again? This search for meaning would eventually determine his life's work.

In the years following liberation, Elie matriculated at several preparatory schools. During this time, he discovered that his two older sisters had survived the Holocaust. They were reunited. Then, he studied at the Sorbonne in Paris. He became a journalist for the French newspaper *L'Arche* and a foreign correspondent for the Israeli newspaper *Yediot Ahronot*. His ability to speak several different languages helped him greatly in these years. He supplemented his small journalist's salary by earning money as a translator for international newspapers. He also taught Hebrew at local schools. This was Wiesel's first foray into teaching, which would become one of his true passions.

As a young journalist, Wiesel covered news and events, but he never spoke or wrote about his experience in the camps. He personally vowed to never speak of it, a vow he kept for ten years after the war. This was partly because there wasn't an audience: people could not yet bring themselves to hear survivors' stories. However, the main reason why Wiesel remained silent was that he felt that words could not do justice to what he had witnessed. To speak of it would be to disrespect or degrade the seriousness of his experience.

Wiesel attended several schools after the war, including the Sorbonne in Paris, France.

FINDING A VOICE

Though able to reintegrate into society, concentration camp survivors had to personally come to terms with what they went through. In the early years, Wiesel never spoke of his experience, but internally he faced a constant battle over what to think about it. Millions of people had lost their lives, and Wiesel lived and worked among people who had failed to step in to stop it. The Holocaust caused a profound crisis of faith, yet he was still a believer. He had to voice these crises of identity in some way.

Finally, in his mid-twenties, Wiesel began speaking out. The year 1955 would mark the ten-year anniversary of his liberation and the end of his self-imposed ten-year period of silence. On a ship back from an assignment in Brazil in 1954, he started putting his experience into words. He wrote an almost nine-hundred-page essay in Yiddish titled *Und di Velt Hot Geshvign* (*And the World Remained Silent*). In his memoir *All Rivers Run to the Sea*, Wiesel describes writing this original manuscript "feverishly" and "breathlessly." He wrote to testify about what happened and to sort out what his survival meant. This version of his story was published in Buenos Aires in 1956 as part of a series of Yiddish memoirs.

It took a fateful encounter for Wiesel's story to become the version we know today. In the early 1950s, Wiesel wanted to get an interview with France's prime minister. While seeking out people who could introduce him to the prime minister, he became acquainted with a special person. That person was François Mauriac. Mauriac, a respected Catholic writer and winner of the Nobel Prize in Literature, was the prime minister's mentor.

In 1955, the two men met and had a conversation about life and faith. Mauriac kept referencing Catholicism and

FRANÇOIS MAURIAC

François Mauriac was born on October 11, 1885, in Bordeaux, France. He was an acclaimed and respected novelist, essayist, poet, playwright, and journalist. A highly decorated public figure in France, Mauriac became a member of the Academie française in 1933. He received the Nobel Prize in Literature in 1952 and was awarded the Grand Cross of the Legion d'honneur in 1958.

Raised in a strict, upper-middle-class family, Mauriac was educated at prominent French universities and then pursued a writing career. Mauriac's first published work was a volume of poems, but he eventually found his true love to be writing novels. He published his first novel, *Young Man in Chains*, in 1913 and spent the rest of his life honing his craft.

continued on page 36

François Mauriac, Wiesel's mentor, colleague, and friend, had a profound impact on his life and literary works.

continued from page 35

His 1932 novel, *Viper's Triangle*, is considered to be his master-piece. He became known for writing about the struggles of modern life within the context of eternity, or the understanding of a higher power. All of his novels feature a religious person coming to terms with sin, grace, and salvation.

Mauriac's interest in these universal human struggles is what drew him to Wiesel's story. He was the major influence on Wiesel's decision to share his story with the world. Mauriac assisted Wiesel in editing and translating *Night* and even wrote the book's foreword. His words are still included in the memoir's most recent editions.

Because he was an adviser to Wiesel and influenced one of the biggest decisions of his life, the two men became more than just colleagues. They remained close friends until Mauriac's death in 1970. Mauriac is remembered today for his prolific writing and contributions to French literature.

how Catholics viewed the suffering of Jesus Christ. This struck a nerve with Wiesel, a man who had suffered unimaginable horrors. His ten years of silence had reached a breaking point. In an interview with the Academy of Achievement, Wiesel explained:

> **When he said "Jesus" again I couldn't take it, and for the only time in my life I was discourteous, which I regret to this day. I said, "Mr. Mauriac...ten years or so ago, I have seen children, hundreds of Jewish children, who suffered more than Jesus did on his cross and we do not speak about it." I felt all of a sudden so embarrassed. I**

**closed my notebook and went to the eleva-
tor. He ran after me. He pulled me back;
he sat down in his chair, and I in mine,
and he began weeping...we stayed there
like that, he weeping and I closed in my
own remorse. And then, at the end...he
simply said, "You know, maybe you should
talk about it."**

This meeting was the encouragement Wiesel needed.
With Mauriac's help, he rewrote his Yiddish book in French
and edited it down to a brief memoir. The title of the book
was *La Nuit* (*Night*). Through spare, straightforward lan-
guage, Wiesel's philosophical writings on the Jewish plight
transformed into a powerful testimony of his time in the concentration camps. *Night* seemed to be a middle ground
between the silence he wanted to keep and the duty he felt he
had, as a survivor, to tell the world what happened. Writing
this book marked the beginning of Wiesel's lifetime of service
in fighting against silence, intolerance, and injustice.

CHAPTER

A MESSENGER SPEAKS

4

In the preface to *Night*'s most recent edition, Wiesel writes that when choosing what to keep and what to eliminate, he focused on substance. He was more concerned about saying too much than saying too little, and he kept this in mind as he condensed the story.

The Holocaust was an extreme example of what happens when hate takes hold and dictates people's actions. However, Wiesel knew that it wasn't the only example. Genocide, injustice, and indifference happened in places around the world. As a Holocaust survivor, Wiesel felt a responsibility to those who perished to share his and their stories with the world. He believed that if people learned the truth about these situations, they couldn't continue to stand by in good conscience and let them happen. Wiesel believed that he could use his story to show what happens when we don't speak up for people in need. He aimed to show the consequences of passivity and the failure to step in when injustices occur.

A QUIET RESPONSE

Confident in his message and bolstered by Mauriac's support, Wiesel sent the manuscript for *Night* to publishing houses in major cities around the world. At the time, all of the major publishers rejected it. A 2008 *New York Times* article references Wiesel's surprise over the publishers' decision, especially since, as Wiesel said, "It was brought to them by François Mauriac, the greatest, greatest writer and journalist in France, a Catholic, a Nobel Prize-winner with all the credentials." Les Éditions de Minuit, a small French publishing house, picked up the book in 1958, but it sold poorly.

Arthur Wang cofounded the American publishing house Hill & Wang in 1956. Wang purchased *Night* in 1959 and published it in 1960.

Across the Atlantic Ocean, Georges Borchardt, Wiesel's literary agent, friend, and fellow Holocaust survivor, shopped *Night* around to the big American publishing houses in 1958 and 1959. The response in the United States was also flat. According to the *New York Times*, Borchardt's explanation for the poor response was: "Nobody really wanted to talk about the Holocaust in those days."

WIESEL'S ADULT LIFE

The 1960s and '70s were a significant time for Wiesel in terms of his personal and professional life. He officially became a U.S. citizen in 1963. He returned to his childhood home in Sighet for the first time in 1964. He met his wife, Marion, and married her in 1969. Three years later, his only child, Shlomo Elisha, was born.

In the late 1960s, Wiesel began lecturing regularly at the 92nd Street Y in Manhattan, and in 1972, he became a distinguished professor of Judaic studies at the City University of New York. In 1976, he transitioned to Boston University, where he became the Andrew W. Mellon Professor in the Humanities. Teaching became one of Wiesel's main passions in life, as he believed that education was critical in preventing injustices from happening in the future. His role as an educator allowed him to reach generations of young people and arm them with awareness of how taking action can prevent tragedy from unfolding. Sensitivity to others, he believed, started with educating others about tolerance.

In addition to teaching, Wiesel spent most of the 1960s and 1970s writing. His books largely focus on the Holocaust, religion, and identity. Many of his books explore the relationships Jews have with God in light of what they, as a group of people, went through. Wiesel's writing includes novels, memoirs, plays, essays, and even children's books. He regards his body of work as a whole unit, with each publication a little piece that contributes to an overall understanding of his philosophy and thoughts on life. He told *Midstream* magazine, "My work has to be seen as an ensemble. Every novel is part of a whole. If you take away one, the edifice will collapse, even the nonfiction." However, none of his other books ever quite reached the level of fame that *Night* achieved.

While trying to get *Night* published, Wiesel had come to the United States on a visa with the idea of working as a correspondent in America. He settled in New York City and began covering events at the United Nations. At first, Wiesel planned on staying in the United States only for the visa's designated amount of time. However, in 1956, he sustained a serious injury when a taxi hit him. His surgery and recovery time put him well past the visa's expiration date. The United States offered him naturalization in order to resolve his status, and he began the process of becoming a citizen.

Wiesel came to the United States as a news correspondent to cover events at the United Nations headquarters in New York City.

Wiesel dedicated the rest of the 1950s to recovering from his injuries, working as a journalist, and making a new life in America. He also devoted a significant amount of his time to writing. Then, in 1959, Hill & Wang, a small American publishing house, bought the *Night* manuscript. Hill & Wang gave Wiesel a $100 advance and published the book in 1960 to positive reviews.

Despite the positive critical response, sales were low, just as in Europe. Of the 3,000 copies published in the initial release, *Night* sold only 1,046 copies in 18 months. Wiesel told the Academy of Achievement that it took three whole years for all of the first-edition copies to sell. This may sound surprising given the book's status as a canonical work of literature, but it took time and a few key events for *Night* to become the world-famous survivor's testimonial that we know today.

OFF THE PAGE AND INTO THE PUBLIC EYE

The publication of *Night* in Argentina, France, and the United States made Wiesel an author by trade. Though *Night* did not immediately fly off the shelves, Wiesel had found his voice and chose to continue telling his story. For himself, Wiesel realized that writing could help him resolve his inner struggle to deal with his experience. For the world, he used the power of the written word to witness and speak out against the Holocaust's atrocities. *Night* sparked the beginning of a prolific literary career: since 1960, he has published over sixty books.

Wiesel published his second book, *Dawn*, in 1961. *Dawn* was a continuation of *Night*. Though it closely reflects Wiesel's own story, this novel is a fictional account of a

Wiesel has written and published numerous books. This photo shows him signing copies of his book *A Beggar in Jerusalem* in 1968.

young Holocaust survivor named Elisha and what he does after being liberated from a concentration camp. This book expresses some of Wiesel's thoughts about the Holocaust, but they are channeled through a fictional character.

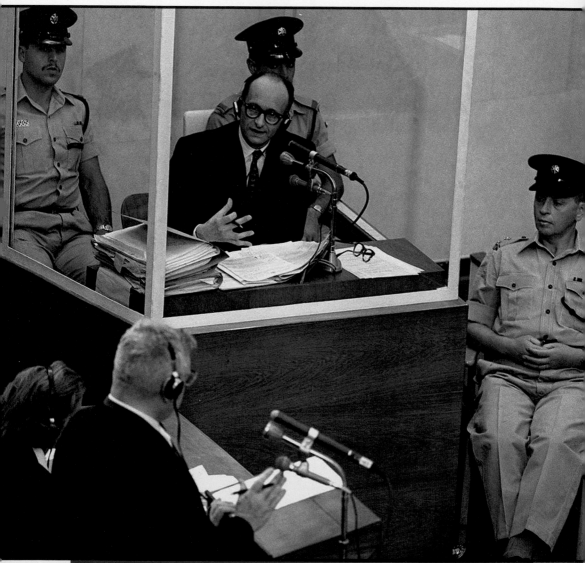

Adolf Eichmann's 1961 trial in Israel brought the Holocaust and Nazi war crimes to the public's attention. Eichmann sat behind protective glass during the trial.

A year later, Wiesel published *Day*. This book also closely resembles Wiesel's story. The main character suffers an injury from a car accident. During his recovery, he comes to terms with the losses he suffered because of the Holocaust. These three literary works are considered to be a trilogy and are often published together to give readers a thorough understanding of a Holocaust survivor's journey from deportation to postwar existence.

Wiesel's books had the potential to be an important vehicle for teaching others about the Holocaust. But as sales from *Night* showed, at the time there wasn't much of an audience for survivors' stories. The Holocaust wasn't studied in schools. In fact, the term "Holocaust" hadn't been widely used at that point. This all changed in 1961, when Adolf Eichmann was tried in Jerusalem and convicted of war crimes against the Jewish people. Eichmann was a Nazi SS officer and one of the key organizers of the Holocaust. He was found guilty of planning and carrying out the deportation of Jews to concentration camps and their massacre there. The Eichmann trial was major international news and caused citizens around the world to finally take notice of the stories survivors had been telling. Wiesel's books, having already been published, were there to meet that need.

CHAPTER 5

THE POWER OF WORDS

The Eichmann trial brought the Holocaust to the world's attention in the 1960s. In the 1970s, increasing conflicts between Israel and several Middle Eastern countries provoked interest in Jewish history. In her essay "The Story of 'Night,'" published in the *New York Times*, Rachel Donadio wrote, "By the early '70s, the Holocaust had become a topic of study in universities, spurred in part by the rise of 'ethnic studies' more generally and a surge of interest in Jewish history after Israel's dramatic military victory in the Israeli-Arab wars of 1967 and 1973."

Wiesel's prominence as an author of Holocaust literature, a professor, and a survivor willing to share his story catapulted him into the public eye. He became the point person for speaking on behalf of survivors and victims. In time, *Night* was elevated to the same level of cultural importance as *The Diary of Anne Frank*. Wiesel had a story, and he had a platform from which to tell it. The only thing left to do was to figure out how to use this opportunity.

RAISING AWARENESS

Wiesel had to ask himself what he wanted to accomplish by becoming an activist. Taking on this responsibility meant that he would speak for millions of people who never had a voice. By sharing his story, he could teach people about what happened. By arming them with knowledge, he could make sure people never turned a blind eye again. He had a chance to prevent atrocities like this from happening again.

Wiesel's guiding philosophy for his activism work was to always keep the victim's plight in mind. He told the Academy of Achievement:

All my adult life, since I began my life as an author, or as a teacher, I always try to listen to the victim. In other words, if I remain silent, I may help my own soul but, because I do not help other people, I poison my soul. Silence never helps the victim. It only helps the victimizer.

Wiesel's compassion for others prompted him to speak out as an activist. The Holocaust was over, and the world was finally studying and understanding the horrors that had happened. Wiesel was there to play his part.

In 1978, U.S. president Jimmy Carter created a special task force to research and investigate the Holocaust. Presidential task forces draw attention to an issue in order to understand it and raise awareness. President Carter appointed Wiesel the chairman of the President's Commission on the Holocaust. Wiesel led the commission

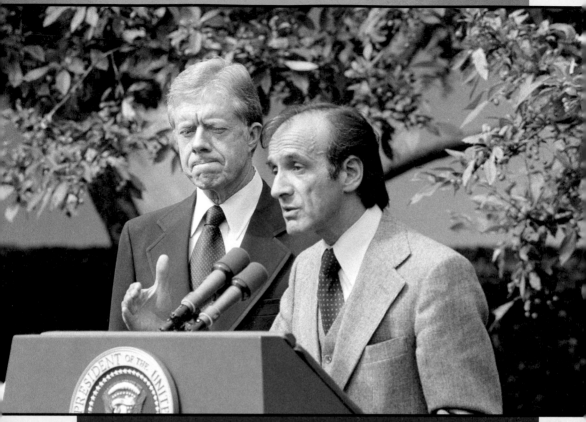

U.S. president Jimmy Carter (*left*) named Wiesel the chairman of the President's Commission on the Holocaust. Wiesel presented the commission's report in the White House Rose Garden on September 27, 1979.

in teaching the world about the Holocaust's victims, survivors, causes and effects, and consequences of inaction.

In his cover letter to the commission's 1979 report, Wiesel explained that the point of the initiative was to fight indifference and apathy. He wrote, "The most vital lesson to be drawn from the Holocaust era is that Auschwitz was possible because the enemy...succeeded in dividing, in separating, in splitting human society, nation against nation, Christian against Jew, young against old. And not enough people cared." These powerful words served as a wake-up call about what can happen when witnesses to evil choose to remain silent.

A year later, in 1980, the U.S. Congress voted unanimously to establish the U.S. Holocaust Memorial Council. This indicated that the commission's work was effective. The council would continue to shine light on the Holocaust, and more and more people in the United States and around the world would become aware of the Holocaust's tragic events. To Wiesel, this was a victory toward his goal of educating others. People would not be able to hide from the past. Rather, they would be equipped to deal with tragic situations that could happen in the future. In essence, his life's work was coming to fruition.

GAINING RECOGNITION

The 1970s and '80s were a time of great progress for Wiesel's work. He was firmly established as a writer; he had almost twenty books published by 1980. *Night* was recognized as an important work of Holocaust literature. The power of its words reached people around the world who may not have understood the true devastation that the Jewish people experienced.

Wiesel was also regarded as a great educator. Having taught full-time at several leading institutions in the 1970s, he began visiting other universities on a part-time basis in the 1980s. He spent the 1982–83 academic year at Yale University as the first Henry Luce Visiting Scholar in Humanities and Social Thought.

Wiesel's work as a Holocaust activist continued to be recognized with prominent awards. In 1980, he received the Prix du Livre Inter from France, a distinguished literary award. He also received the S. Y. Agnon Medal and the Jabotinsky Medal in recognition of his writing from the state of Israel.

A NOBEL LAUREATE FOR PEACE

Wiesel has received countless awards, honors, and honorary degrees and has held prominent positions as a result of his dedication to speaking out against indifference and injustice. However, there is one award that stands out from all the others in terms of its prestige and importance: the Nobel Peace Prize.

Wiesel was awarded the Nobel Prize for Peace on December 10, 1986. He is pictured receiving the award with his son (*left*) and Nobel Prize Committee chairman Egil Aarvik (*right*).

The Nobel Peace Prize is awarded each year to people or organizations who have "done the most or the best work for fraternity between nations, for the abolition or reduction of standing armies, and for the holding and promotion of peace congresses."

Wiesel received this award in 1986. Calling him a "messenger to mankind," the Nobel Prize Committee said that Wiesel's message of peace and human dignity was not limited to the plight of Jewish people only, but that it embraced all oppressed people and races. It said his testimony about the Holocaust represented a lifelong effort to believe that "forces fighting evil in the world can be victorious." It was for these reasons that Wiesel was deemed worthy of one of the world's highest honors.

In his acceptance speech, Wiesel spoke directly to victims of human rights violations all over the world. He promised victims of injustice, indifference, and genocide that they would not be alone or forgotten. His life's work both before and after receiving the Nobel Prize has proved time and again the strength of his commitment to his beliefs.

In 1985, U.S. president Ronald Reagan presented Wiesel with the Congressional Gold Medal of Achievement in honor of his life's work. He was recognized for bringing the Holocaust to the world's attention, dedicating his life to memorializing victims, and ensuring that future generations would not let something like the Holocaust happen again. When presenting the award to Wiesel, President Reagan remarked:

Elie Wiesel has helped make the memory of the Holocaust eternal by preserving

the story of the six million Jews in his works. Like the Prophets whose words guide to this day, his works will teach humanity timeless lessons. He teaches about despair but also about hope. He teaches about our capacity to do evil but also about the possibility of courage and resistance and about our capacity to sacrifice for a higher good. He teaches about death. But in the end, he teaches about life.

When he received the Congressional Gold Medal in 1985, Wiesel urged President Ronald Reagan (*left*) not to visit the military cemetery in Bitburg, Germany. Here, the two shake hands as Vice President George Bush (*center*) looks on.

Wiesel was deeply honored to receive this award and accepted it with the utmost gratitude. He did, however, use his time in front of a national audience as a teaching opportunity. He used his speech to speak out against President Reagan's planned visit to Bitburg Cemetery, the site of thousands of SS guard graves. He implored the president not to go, arguing that visiting a Nazi burial site would be offensive to Holocaust survivors, victims, and the Jewish population.

Wiesel's public plea to the president of the United States drew others' attention to the issue. Several U.S. congressmen signed petitions against the visit. Popular musical artists such as the Ramones and Frank Zappa recorded songs in protest. Though the vocal dissent did not prevent the president from visiting the site, the support for the dissenters demonstrated that the world had compassion for the Holocaust victims. This was exactly what Wiesel had tried to achieve through his writing and teaching efforts.

A LIFETIME OF SERVICE

Human rights violations have occurred in every era of history. Holocaust education does not singlehandedly prevent other instances of genocide or injustice from taking place. Because injustices still occur and because there are always victims who need a voice, Wiesel has used his fame to speak up for those who cannot do so themselves. Remembering how lonely he felt during the darkest moments of his life, he has pledged never to let other victims of such tragedies feel so alone and powerless again. In his adult life, he has spoken up and become active for several different causes.

THE ELIE WIESEL FOUNDATION FOR HUMANITY

The 1990s and 2000s have demonstrated Wiesel's commitment to Holocaust awareness, the Jewish cause, and the plight of suffering people around the world. Wiesel has said repeatedly that it is his moral obligation to honor the memory of genocide victims. He does this today, even in his late

eighties, by paying attention to witness and survival testi-
monials, advocating for recognition, and promoting
education.

Wiesel and his wife, Marion, established the Elie Wiesel Foundation
for Humanity to advocate for education, tolerance, and justice
around the world.

In 1988, Wiesel and his wife, Marion, established the Elie Wiesel Foundation for Humanity. They formed the foundation to teach people of all ages how to combat indifference, intolerance, and injustice. Since its creation, the foundation and its members have worked to promote acceptance, understanding, and equality among all people. They do this by running youth-focused programs and starting dialogues in classrooms and other educational environments. The foundation's mission demonstrates Wiesel's commitment to using education to reach young people in order to make the world a better place. Launching the foundation with his wife gave Wiesel another platform from which to convey his message. Because he and Marion lead the nonprofit, he is able to focus the organization's work on the causes closest to his heart and his life's mission.

Jewish-related causes are very important to Wiesel. He ensures that a significant portion of the foundation's efforts go toward promoting causes that fall into that category. For example, the foundation runs the Beit Tzipora Centers for Study and Enrichment in Israel. These educational centers help Ethiopian Jewish children overcome inequalities in their education. The opportunities the children gain from their involvement with the Beit Tzipora Centers allow them to integrate more fully into Israeli society, as well as receive help with their studies. The centers also provide support for any emotional or social issues the children may face.

In addition to using his foundation to help people, Wiesel uses it as a vehicle to publicly condemn atrocities that have occured around the world. In 2007, the Elie Wiesel Foundation published an open letter to Turkey, calling for the nation to acknowledge an event in its history that could be considered genocide: the mass killing

IN THE FOOTSTEPS OF ELIE WIESEL

In 1997, Wiesel worked with an initiative called the Elie Wiesel Project to speak out against indifference. Using the Holocaust as a teaching tool, he gave a speech in front of twenty-three thousand people in Charlotte, North Carolina, on the moral importance of compassion and justice. Inspired by his visit and the project's call to action, Wiesel offered his own money and time to develop programs that would uphold these ideals. Today, it is called the Echo Foundation.

In 2007, the Echo Foundation produced a film called *In the Footsteps of Elie Wiesel*. The film follows twelve American high school students as they retrace Wiesel's path from his childhood home to the concentration camps. The film shows the students coming to terms with the Holocaust's evil and seeing firsthand the consequences of silence and indifference. By the end of the film, the students show us, the viewers, that it is our responsibility to create a just and humane world. They demonstrate that education and awareness can go a long way in making the world safe for all people.

Wiesel still works closely with the Echo Foundation today. It is just one more example of how Wiesel has used his story to teach young people an important universal lesson.

and deportation of Armenian citizens from 1918 to 1923. The letter, signed by 53 Nobel laureates, supported a study from 2003 that said the slaughter of nearly 1.5 million Armenians should be considered genocide, based on the internationally accepted definition. The letter brought visibility to a controversial issue and furthered Wiesel's life mission to speak out for voiceless victims.

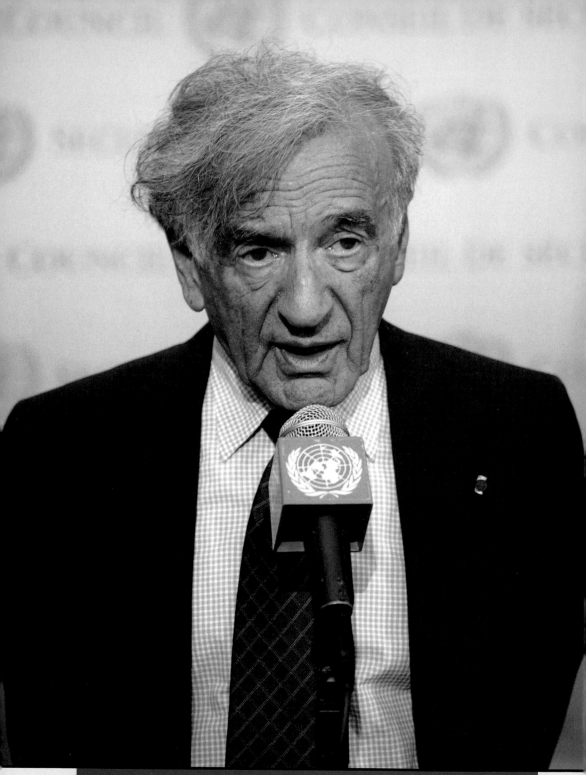

Wiesel has continued his advocacy work throughout his adult life. In 2006, he addressed the United Nations about the humanitarian crisis in Darfur, Africa.

A LASTING LEGACY

Wiesel dedicated his adult life to promoting compassion and justice across several platforms. *Night* grew in prominence over more than fifty years to become the paradigm of a Holocaust survivor testimonial. His legacy has only been furthered by his commitment to activism and willingness to fight for causes he believes in.

Though he has always been a prominent figure, Wiesel's well-established fame reignited in 2006, when Oprah Winfrey chose *Night* as a selection for her book club. Winfrey, one of the most famous talk-show hosts in the world, said when she announced her selection that Wiesel's book should be "required reading for all humanity." Sales of *Night* soared following her announcement. Between 2006 and 2011, 2,021,000 copies sold, effectively making the book a *New York Times* best seller. Wiesel had found a new audience with which to share his story. He went on a televised return trip to Auschwitz to teach a new generation of readers about his experiences and the importance of fighting for justice and tolerance.

The rest of the 2000s were just as important in Wiesel's fight for humanitarian causes. In 2006, he appeared before the United Nations Security Council to lobby for action in Darfur, a country in Africa whose people were under the oppressive thumb of a genocidal regime. In 2012, Wiesel made headlines because he publicly gave up a medal given to him by the Hungarian government eight years earlier. After Hungarian government officials took part in a ceremony honoring a writer with Nazi connections, he took this action to protest their "whitewashing...of criminal episodes that happened during the Holocaust." These are

Elie Wiesel and President Barack Obama visited Buchenwald in 2009. They embraced after Wiesel's memorial speech.

only a few examples of how Wiesel has used his public visibility to draw attention to causes and effect change.

Today, in his late eighties, Wiesel is an old man, but his life of activism continues. For decades he has fought tirelessly for his commitment to social justice and moral responsibility. Whether it is using his own experiences in the Holocaust to educate generations far removed from that time period or raising awareness of humanitarian issues that plague us today, Elie Wiesel has become a hero, a voice, and a spokesperson for millions of innocent people around the globe.

Timeline

September 30, 1928 Elie Wiesel is born in Sighet, Transylvania.

January 30, 1933 Adolf Hitler is appointed chancellor of Germany by German president Paul Von Hindenberg.

September 15, 1935 Nazi officials decree the Nuremberg Race Laws, denying Jews their German citizenship.

September 1, 1939 Germany invades Poland, starting World War II.

May 1944 Wiesel and his family are deported from Sighet to Auschwitz. Wiesel's mother and youngest sister are killed upon arrival.

January 1945 Shlomo Wiesel dies of dysentery in the infirmary of Buchenwald, a concentration camp in Germany.

April 11, 1945 Allied forces liberate the Buchenwald concentration camp. Wiesel is finally free.

May 7–8, 1945 Germany surrenders to Allied forces.

1948 Wiesel is reunited with his two surviving sisters. He enrolls at the Sorbonne in Paris, France.

1952 Wiesel becomes a reporter for an international newspaper that takes him on assignments around the world.

1954–1955 Wiesel writes a nearly nine-hundred-page memoir of his experiences in Yiddish. He meets François Mauriac and is persuaded to share his story with the world. Wiesel edits the material and translates it into French.

1956 Wiesel is struck by a taxi in New York City. The accident forces him to stay in the United States past his visa's expiration date, leading him to become a U.S. citizen.

1958 *La Nuit* (*Night*) is published in France.

1960 Hill & Wang publishes *Night* in the United States.

1961 *Dawn*, the follow-up book to *Night*, is published.

1962 *Day* is published, completing the trilogy of books about Wiesel's Holocaust experience.

May 31, 1962 Former Nazi leader Adolf Eichmann is executed for his role as one of the architects of the Holocaust, bringing that period of history to the world's attention.

1969 Wiesel marries his wife, Marion. She later becomes the translator for most of his writings.

1972 Wiesel's son, Shlomo Elisha, is born.

1978 U.S. president Jimmy Carter appoints Wiesel chairman of the newly formed President's Commission on the Holocaust.

April 19, 1985 U.S. president Ronald Reagan presents Wiesel with the Congressional Gold Medal of Achievement.

October 14, 1986 Wiesel is named the winner of the Nobel Peace Prize.

April 22, 1993 The U.S. Holocaust Memorial Museum opens, fulfilling a recommendation made by the President's Commission on the Holocaust in 1978.

2006 Oprah Winfrey chooses *Night* as a selection for her book club. Sales soar and put Wiesel's work on the *New York Times* best-seller list.

2007 The Echo Foundation produces the documentary film *In the Footsteps of Elie Wiesel.*

2012 Wiesel returns an award he received from Hungary in 2004. He does this to protest Hungarian officials' participation in honoring a writer who was part of a Nazi-affiliated group.

Glossary

ANTI-SEMITIC Exhibiting hostility to or prejudice against Jews.

APATHY A lack of interest or concern.

ATROCITY An act of extreme cruelty, especially against civilians or prisoners during wartime.

CANONICAL Of or relating to a group of literary works that are traditionally considered to be very important.

CONDEMN To express complete disapproval of, usually in a public forum.

CREMATORIUM A place where a deceased person's body is burned.

DEPORT To remove someone forcibly from a country.

DISSENT Public disagreement with an official opinion, decision, or policy.

EMACIATED Abnormally thin or weak, usually because of sickness or lack of food.

FRUITION The point at which a plan or project is realized.

GENOCIDE The deliberate killing of a large group of people, especially those of a particular ethnic group or nation.

GESTAPO The German secret police during the Nazi era.

GHETTO The Jewish quarter of a city under Nazi occupation where all Jews were forced to live, typically in overcrowded conditions and separate from the rest of the population.

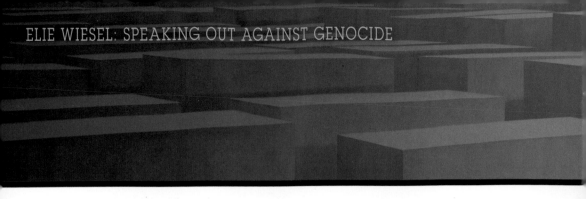

IRREFUTABLE Impossible to deny or disprove.

LIBERATE To give liberty to; to set free.

MATRICULATE To enroll in a college or university.

NAZISM A body of political beliefs held and put into effect in Germany in the 1930s and 1940s under the dictatorship of Adolf Hitler. Its doctrines included racist nationalism, expansionism, totalitarianism, and anti-Semitism.

ORTHODOX Strictly keeping to traditional religious doctrines and rituals.

PARADIGM An example that serves as a model or standard.

PROLIFIC Producing many works.

REGIME A government, especially an authoritarian one.

SCHUTZSTAFFEL (SS) A paramilitary organization under the Nazi regime that protected high-ranking German officials, ran concentration camp operations, and carried out Hitler's genocidal plan against Jews.

SECULAR Nonreligious.

TESTIMONIAL A statement that serves as evidence in support of a particular truth, fact, or claim.

YESHIVA A traditional Jewish school devoted mainly to the study of rabbinic literature and the Talmud.

For More Information

Association of Holocaust Organizations
P.O. Box 230317
Hollis, NY 11423
(516) 582-4571
Website: http://www.ahoinfo.org
Established in 1985, this organization serves as an international network for organizations and individuals working to advance Holocaust education, remembrance, and research.

Canadian Jewish Congress Charities Committee
    National Archives (CJCCC)
1590 Docteur Penfield Avenue
Montreal, QC H3G 1C5
Canada
(514) 931-7531
Website: http://www.cjccc.ca
The CJCCC National Archives collect and preserve documentation on all aspects of the Jewish presence in Quebec and Canada. Collections cover topics including immigration, integration into Canadian society, community organization, discrimination, oppressed Jewry in other countries, education, literature, and genealogy.

The Echo Foundation
1125 E. Morehead Street, Suite 101

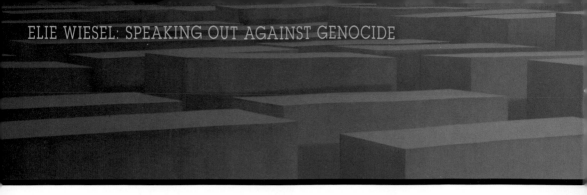

Charlotte, NC 28204
(704) 347-3844
Website: http://www.echofoundation.org
The Echo Foundation is a nonprofit organization that
promotes education on racial diversity, culture, and
tolerance via workshops, talks, and various educational programs.

The Elie Wiesel Foundation for Humanity
555 Madison Avenue
New York, NY 10022
(212) 490-7788
Website: http://www.eliewieselfoundation.org
The Elie Wiesel Foundation for Humanity is a nonprofit
organization that works to combat indifference, intolerance, and injustice through youth-focused
educational programs.

Facing History and Ourselves
16 Hurd Road
Brookline, MA 02445-6919
(800) 856-9039
Website: http://www.facinghistory.org
This organization works to combat racism, anti-
Semitism, and prejudice and nurtures democracy
through education programs worldwide. By teaching
the development of the Holocaust and other

examples of genocide, it helps students make the connection between history and the moral choices they confront in their own lives.

National Holocaust Monument
c/o Development Council
49 Hearthstone Crescent
Toronto, ON M24 162
Canada
(416) 636-5225
Website: http://www.holocaustmonument.ca
The official Canadian memorial to the Holocaust, the National Holocaust Monument honors victims and survivors who have made contributions to Canadian society. The memorial is slated to open in 2015.

USC Shoah Foundation
The Institute for Visual History and Education
Leavey Library
650 West 35th Street, Suite 114
Los Angeles, CA 90089
Website: http://sfi.usc.edu
(213) 740-6001
The Shoah Foundation is dedicated to making audiovisual interviews with survivors and witnesses of the Holocaust and other genocides around the world.

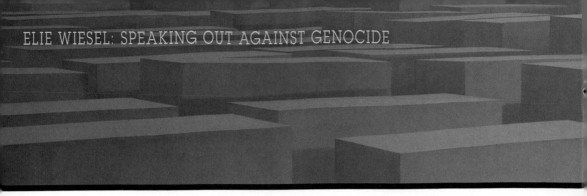

U.S. Holocaust Memorial Museum
100 Raoul Wallenberg Place SW
Washington, DC 20024-2126
(202) 488-0400
Website: http://www.ushmm.org
The U.S. Holocaust Memorial Museum is the United States'
    official Holocaust memorial. The museum handles
    projects related to the documentation, interpretation,
    and study of Holocaust history. It sponsors on-site and
    traveling exhibitions, educational outreach, and
    Holocaust commemorations, including the nation's
    annual observance of the Days of Remembrance in the
    U.S. Capitol.

WEBSITES

Due to the changing nature of Internet links, Rosen Publishing
has developed an online list of websites related to the subject
of this book. This site is updated regularly. Please use this link
to access the list:

http://www.rosenlinks.com/DHH/Wiesel

For Further Reading

Arato, Rona. *The Last Train: A Holocaust Story.* Toronto, Canada: Owlkids, 2013.

Boas, Jacob. *We Are Witnesses: Five Diaries of Teenagers Who Died in the Holocaust.* New York, NY: Square Fish Books, 2009.

Buergenthal, Thomas. *A Lucky Child: A Memoir of Surviving Auschwitz as a Young Boy.* New York, NY: Hachette Book Group, 2009.

Byers, Ann. *Courageous Teen Resisters: Primary Sources from the Holocaust.* Berkeley Heights, NJ: Enslow Publishers, 2010.

Byers, Ann. *Trapped—Youth in the Nazi Ghettos: Primary Sources from the Holocaust.* Berkeley Heights, NJ: Enslow Publishers, 2010.

Dakers, Diane. *Elie Wiesel: Holocaust Survivor and Messenger for Humanity.* New York, NY: Crabtree Publishing, 2012.

Darman, Peter. *The Holocaust and Life Under Nazi Occupation.* New York, NY: Rosen Publishing Group, 2012.

Deem, James M. *Auschwitz: Voices from the Death Camp.* Berkeley Heights, NJ: Enslow Publishers, 2011.

Down, Susan Brophy. *Irena Sendler: Bringing Life to Children of the Holocaust.* New York, NY: Crabtree Publishing, 2012.

Frank, Anne. *Anne Frank: The Diary of a Young Girl.* New York, NY: Doubleday, 1967.

Freeman, Charles. *Why Did the Rise of the Nazis Happen?* New York, NY: Gareth Stevens Publishing, 2010.

Kor, Eva, and Lisa Rojany-Buccieri. *Surviving the Angel of Death: The True Story of a Mengele Twin in Auschwitz.* Terre Haute, IN: Tanglewood Publishing, 2009.

Rappaport, Doreen. *Beyond Courage: The Untold Story of Jewish Resistance During the Holocaust.* Somerville, MA: Candlewick Press, 2012.

Sheehan, Sean. *Why Did the Holocaust Happen?* New York, NY: Gareth Stevens Publishing, 2010.

Wein, Elizabeth. *Code Name Verity.* New York, NY: Hyperion Books, 2012.

Wiesel, Elie. *Dawn,* New York, NY: Hill & Wang, 1961.

Wiesel, Elie. *Day.* New York, NY: Hill & Wang, 1962.

Wiesel, Elie. *Night.* New York, NY: Hill & Wang, 1960.

Zullo, Allan. *Escape: Children of the Holocaust.* New York, NY: Scholastic, 2011.

Bibliography

American Academy of Achievement. "Elie Wiesel Interview." June 29, 1996. Retrieved May 10, 2013 (http://www.achievement.org/autodoc/page/wie0int-1).

American-Israeli Cooperative Enterprise. "Elie Wiesel (1928–)." Jewish Virtual Library, 2013. Retrieved July 25, 2013 (http://www.jewishvirtuallibrary.org/jsource/biography/Wiesel.html).

BBC Tyne. "Non-Jewish Holocaust Victims: The 5,000,000 Others." BBC.co.uk, April 21, 2006. Retrieved January 3, 2014 (http://www.bbc.co.uk/tyne/content/articles/2005/01/20/holocaust_memorial_other_victims_feature.shtml).

Biography.com. "Elie Wiesel Biography—Facts, Birthday, Life Story." 2013. Retrieved May 20, 2013 (http://www.biography.com/people/elie-wiesel-9530714).

Boog, Jason. "Oprah Winfrey Closes Her TV Book Club." *GalleyCat*, May 25, 2011. Retrieved August 15, 2013 (http://www.mediabistro.com/galleycat/top-10-bestselling-books-in-oprahs-book-club_b30637).

Danielyan, Emil. "Nobel Laureates Call for Armenian-Turkish Reconciliation." Radio Free Europe/Radio Liberty, April 10, 2007. Retrieved August 15, 2013 (http://www.rferl.org/content/article/1075779.html).

Donadio, Rachel. "The Story of 'Night.'" *New York Times*, January 20, 2008. Retrieved June 20, 2013

(http://www.nytimes.com/2008/01/20/books/
review/Donadio-t.html).

The Echo Foundation. "In the Footsteps of Elie
Wiesel." 2009. Retrieved July 3, 2013 (http://
www.inthefootstepsofeliewiesel.org).

The Elie Wiesel Foundation for Humanity. "About Us."
Retrieved July 3, 2013 (http://www.eliewieselfoundation
.org/aboutus.aspx).

Franklin, Ruth. "A Thousand Darknesses." *New Republic*
Online, March 23, 2006. Retrieved August 2, 2013
(http://www.powells.com/review/2006_03_23.html).

Heffner, Richard. "A Conversation with Elie Wiesel—
Richard Heffner's Open Mind—THIRTEEN." Thirteen.
org, April 7, 2008. Retrieved January 3, 2014 (http://
www.thirteen.org/openmind/civil-rights/a
-conversation-with-elie-wiesel/1829/#).

Henry, Gary. "Gary Henry on Transcendence in
Wiesel's Work." In *Elie Wiesel's Night*, edited by
Harold Bloom, 66–76. New York, NY: Infobase
Publishing, 2009.

Lowin, Joseph. "A Conversation with Elie Wiesel." *Midstream*,
March/April 2006. Retrieved August 10, 2013 (http://
www.midstreamthf.com/200603/feature.html).

NobelPrize.org. "Press Release—Peace 1986." October
14, 1986. Retrieved August 20, 2013 (http://www
.nobelprize.org/nobel_prizes/peace/laureates/
1986/press.html).

Oprah.com. "Inside Auschwitz." May 24, 2006. Retrieved July 3, 2013 (http://www.oprah.com/world/Inside-Auschwitz).

PBS.org. "Elie Wiesel: First Person Singular." October 24, 2002. Retrieved May 10, 2013 (http://www.pbs.org/eliewiesel/index.html).

PBS.org. "Wiesel Resources: Remarks on Presenting the Congressional Gold Medal to Elie Wiesel and on Signing the Jewish Heritage Week Proclamation, April 19, 1985." 2002. Retrieved August 1, 2013 (http://www.pbs.org/eliewiesel/resources/reagan.html).

Simpson, Daniel. "Sighet Journal; Elie Wiesel Asks a Haunted Hometown to Face Up." *New York Times*, July 31, 2002. Retrieved January 30, 2014 (http://www.nytimes.com/2002/07/31/world/sighet-journal-elie-wiesel-asks-a-haunted-hometown-to-face-up.html).

U.S. Holocaust Memorial Museum. "Auschwitz." June 10, 2013. Retrieved January 3, 2014 (http://www.ushmm.org/wlc/en/article.php?ModuleId=10005189).

U.S. Holocaust Memorial Museum. "Hungary After the German Occupation." June 10, 2013. Retrieved May 10, 2013 (http://www.ushmm.org/wlc/en/article.php?ModuleId=10005458).

Wiesel, Elie. *All Rivers Run to the Sea: Memoirs*. New York, NY: Schocken Books, 1995.

Wiesel, Elie. "Cover Letter to the Report: President's Commission on the Holocaust, September 27, 1979." U.S. Holocaust Memorial Museum. Retrieved July 25, 2013 (http://www.ushmm.org/information/about -the-museum/presidents-commission/cover-letter).

Wiesel, Elie. *Night*. New York, NY: Hill & Wang, 1960.

Winfrey, Oprah. "Oprah Talks to Elie Wiesel." Oprah .com. Retrieved July 31, 2013 (http://www.oprah .com/omagazine/Oprah-Interviews-Elie-Wiesel/1).

Wyatt, Edward. "Oprah's Book Club Turns to Elie Wiesel." *New York Times*, January 16, 2006. Retrieved July 31, 2013 (http://www.nytimes.com/2006/01/ 16/books/16cnd-oprah.html).

Index

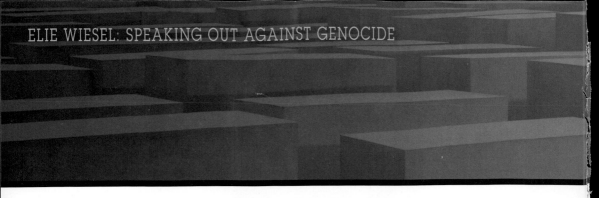

ABOUT THE AUTHOR

Sarah Machajewski is an author, editor, and journalist who specializes in nonfiction educational materials for children and young adults. She writes on a variety of subjects but is particularly interested in historical topics. Machajewski graduated from the University of Pittsburgh in 2010 with a bachelor's degree in English literature and history. Her professional writing experience and educational background lend a unique perspective to her works, which now include more than two hundred books on science, math, literature, and history.

PHOTO CREDITS